Earth, My Witness

poems by

Magdalena Montagne

Finishing Line Press
Georgetown, Kentucky

Earth, My Witness

ACKNOWLEDGMENTS

Some of these poems were originally published in the following journals and
anthologies:

If the Sky Was My Heart: California Poets in the Schools Statewide Anthology:
"Poem is Banquet, Poem is Feast"

La Gazette: "First Day of Summer"

Manzanita Quarterly: "Making Love to Oak"

One Hundred Parades: California Poets in the Schools Statewide Anthology:
"Thinking of Saint Francis"

Porter Gulch Review: "Communion," "Before Work," "Where Sorrow Lives,"
"Learning to Speak Poetry"

Publisher: Leah Maines
Editor: Christen Kincaid
Cover Art: Sajid Martin
Author Photo: Lynn Rebbeck
Cover Design: Elizabeth Maines McCleavy

Order online: www.finishinglinepress.com
         also available on amazon.com

Author inquiries and mail orders:
Finishing Line Press
P. O. Box 1626
Georgetown, Kentucky 40324
U. S. A.

Table of Contents

Into

*To my daughter, Isabelle, for light and wonder and joy;
and to my husband, Steve, for your love and unwavering support
of truth and poetry, and for everything.*

Initiation

Sonnet for My Tormentor

I envy the broad sweep of the owl
Whose nocturnal destination is joy
Escaping nightmare's gray and lonely scowl
The silent chase of an unchaste boy
He pinned me to the darkest plot of earth
My lovely soul distracted rose above
The likes of him, so hurt and hurt and hurt
Releasing me to sorrow, a mourning dove
What happened in a room too small to stay
Coy his moves, his giant unmade bed
I erased him with a bigger world each day
Wished him, wished him, wished him dead and dead.
       I'd almost forgotten the flesh and kick of it
       The orange cat a flash of memory lit
       Cried the whole time, brought me back—unfit.

Nightmare Ritual at Eleven

When he entered me
without permission
I could only wonder
at what words I would say.
Afterwards
red blood leaves
on the maple
outside my room
my only witness.
Nothing stirred then
except for an occasional
ripple of wind.
A warning.
It took years for me to decode this language.
To say what he trespassed against.
Interloper
Dumb animal
After his prey.

Mother's Crying Song

Mother's cries down the hallway
so deep and wide, a river I could not swim.
So landed, I understood suddenly
the darkness I was born into.
Chasing the angels of light
my entire life
to garner forgiveness.
But the score remains unbalanced, uneven:
heave, a sob, in my direction
a scar, a wound
wailing and lamentation
I still hear
when night cracks me open
into pieces.

Hummingbirds

Unpredictable as wind
they alight momentarily at the feeder.

For sugar water sustenance they wait and flutter,
awkward and nervous, without the grace of slow-moving doves.

Rainbow dressed they catch the sun
as I, phantom weary, watch them turn and go.

O nonsensical birds with your dagger swords
capable of prying nectar from unsuspecting lavender
and lilies in the meadows below.

Baby birds, smaller than a thimble,
my mother enjoined me to use.

An armor to protect a daughter's nimble fingers
for the womanly task of mending

that which was sheer and fragile.
Hopeless beyond repair.
.
Hapless, I spilled blood for her.
Just so she would know
I was made of flesh—real.

Last Breath

I was not there to see my mother take her last breath—
slow coil of exhale moving out into the stratosphere.

The heavens resting lightly on earth,
just that time of morning.

Close to the hour of my birth
first delight of air.

She gave me breath
and later admonished me with it.

The particles elongated to become
fright and scream, not the universal sound of aum.

Now she is wordless.

Decay weighs.
They fix her up.

The corpse rotting already,
but hair and nails still growing steadily.

My sisters pick out something nice for her to wear to casket.
Someone muses over hair and makeup.
Why bother with these exhausting decisions?

I'll choose cremation.
The dust of my flesh and bones

a fine powder
to spill out
over everyone.

The Day After My Mother is Buried

I awake to the sight of six adolescent male deer
their antlers beginning to bud out.
Stalwart brothers in undulating procession
heading toward my yard.

They move peacefully.
Silent as pall bearers.
As if rehearsed,
sidestepping each other.

They look to the garden fence
they could easily vault over.
Provocation of swollen tomatoes
and sweet peas on the vine.

But they move on
toward the meadow and the brambles
as the day stretches out her arms
thin and fragile through fog.

I'd follow them too
if I knew
I could leave my grief
in that open field.

Along with half-eaten blackberries
delicate and bruised.
Juice still dripping
from our open mouths.

Two Years After She is Gone

In Santa Cruz spring is like persistent good news,
blossoms awash in flame on mock plum and cherries.

Days reaching wholeheartedly their zenith,
restoring equilibrium as night recedes further and further.

And what of my mother's body now, I wonder?
For two long years buried in earth.

Shakes me hard to realize I don't know where she's buried,
Heaven's Gate or Angel of Mercy?

No matter I wouldn't much appreciate which path to take—
to finally arrive at a bouquet of plastic flowers
or one lone wild rose.

It's a mystery that our corpses decompose.
Seemingly indestructible bodies chewed away,
collapsing like ruins or towers or holes

in rich brown loam
turned muddy in Jersey spring.

Afterthought

I had almost forgotten the sound of rain
after another dusty summer.
A season that stretched long
from April to November.

Crowning the browning hillsides,
covering the deceptively abundant valley floor
with sticky artichoke globes, spikes of broccoli florets,
growing on false promises, a faltering aquifer.

I ran out into the twilight evening,
feeling the waves of it come down.
And the scent that rose up
drove me back to Jersey cement blacktop,
cooling the streets and playground.

Summer rain ending my child-games,
hopscotch and colored chalk,
fading mauve and green.

And my mother's voice calling, *come inside now.*
And calling again, *come inside.*
Until at last I had the sense to listen.

I remember my mother now,
straining to hear her voice again.
Who did not love the rain
but was eager for the flowers.
Yellow and red roses her favorites,
long stemmed in bright vases.

I imagine the flowers
with their delicate upturned faces.
Gloom of dust dispelled.

And if they could turn, if they could speak,
I could hear them say, "Hallelujah!"
Loud enough to raise my mother
from her dead sleep in the earth.

White Dwarfs and Black Holes

Today I am empty of wishes.
Like rock, sedated by Time.
My genius brain unwinds.
Spooling out memories in reverse:

Not a garden.
Not a raven with its slick black feathers.
Not church or the circus slide.
The juggler's choreography in air, the curious clown.

Not the game at the fair
where you toss a ball into a bucket,
only to come up
empty-handed.

My mother sang a song about wishing on a star
and I thought she meant it.
The constellations more real
than the haze of morning.

Bacon frying noisily in a pan,
eggs poaching rapidly.
She'd rather have been consuming
opera and poetry, than bearing three children.

Two already a burden,
and I'm the third, unholy trinity.

I got that from her,
that wishes make you stupid, really.

She settled with my father
the least of all evils.
Considered all desires dangerous,
supplanted them with prayer.

A wish taken to the next level.
In His hands.

A stunning woman throws three coins in a fountain.
Brilliant.
But that was Hollywood, 1954.
And here we are, back at stars,

The view from the back seat of our family's black Buick.
We're travelling, I don't know where…
Underneath the night sky of Andromeda, Cassiopeia, Pegasus

painted across the New York skyline.
Sparkling like the lights at Christmas.

My father on the couch at home, without us.
Drinking a Mai Tai or a Screwdriver
depending on his mood, the season.

It's solstice now.
And the sky is rich, heavy with stars.
And you mother are closer to me than ever.

Having entered the rush of Eternity,
your unspoken wishes tug and pull at my heart.

Where Sorrow Lives

Sorrow lives in my mother's kitchen
polished clean
scrubbed with the force of a woman
who is wounded and fighting
with all her might.
Sorrow lives

between the matching Lenox china
and the freshly pressed linens.
Let me lie down with this sorrow
her prayer.

Sorrow lives in the basement
where my father labored
with the skill saw, hammer and nails.

The time he lopped off a finger
sorrow sang.
But usually she hummed gently in the background
through the leaves of autumn swaying
radiating like the ping pinging of the sideboard heater
snowy winters.

Sorrow lives in the ancient apple trees in the yard
where even the blood red
of the gladiolas my father planted
could not spirit it away.

Or obscure the history of the man who groomed the horses
who hanged himself finally from the rafters of the barn
where the ponies stood

ready to warm him
with breath
fresh with the hay he had just offered.

Sorrow lives in the church
we visited on Sundays.
At the altar
with the statue of Jesus.

In the rusty nails straight through the hands and feet
and the cold tears shed
at the crucifixion
when he felt abandoned by his own Father.

Sorrow lives quietly
for three days
in the tomb
and rises again

Spreading like wildfire
smoke and ashes and dust
in our mouths
soundless and wordless

in what we cannot say
sorrow lives.

And she's in my sisters
behind their eyes and the crook of my neck
and underneath our fingernails.
In the most intimate of places.

How can we turn our backs on sorrow's seduction?
So we succumb
to her lamentations
and weeping.

She is shrouded
in a veil.
She is vain.
She is sometimes sleeping.

In my sister's
days in bed.
There she is,
sorrow.

Day after day
My sister flirts with sorrow.
Until she cannot get breath—almost loses consciousness
becomes ecstatic with sorrow.

Sorrow and my own anger
both rise.
Twin flames in a frosty glass,
a porch light dim on a starless night.

Talisman

When I see my mother
she is holding a rosary.
Heavy black beads, not worn, but solid
despite years of repetition.
Eternal *Hail Marys* and *Our Fathers.*
And the small in-between prayers
I can no longer remember.

My father's mother too
had this talisman.
Wore them on her belt
like a nun in an abbey.
Murmuring incantations
in Italian.

My mother warned me to stay clear.
The evil eye upon us.
The power of the charm
that hung around my grandmother's neck
sharing a small space
with Jesus on the cross
and a locket with my father's picture—
her only son.

When my mother was mugged
I had already left home.
Stopped being Catholic.
Her black Cadillac newly parked
garage gloomy Jersey winter.
The young man who came at her with a knife
took the purse she always carried
a rosary concealed.

We didn't speak much then.
But as soon as I heard
I bought her an amethyst talisman.
Offered it as reparation
for my sins and the sins of all sinners.

The gift went unnoticed.
The way my prayers weren't heard then either.

But my sisters and I prayed anyway
in the church where we had grown
into blasphemous women
in my mother's eyes.
Prayed she would not die.
That she would not leave us
before we could be born fully.

I still carry a rosary.
Not the first one
I received on confirmation eve,
but a pearlescent silver strand
I picked up at a thrift store
or a yard sale, unblessed, not yet holy.

Especially on planes
I pull them out.
Sweating the beads through fervent fingers.
And when walking into the black pitch of night—
eying the flickering shadows of the man who beat my mother.
My father's eyes stark and dilated with liquor.

My first boyfriend taunted me.
Refuted the very idea of prayer.
I persisted,
then disappeared.

Became a Buddhist easily.
Carrying a new invocation.
Beads that I wear.
The mala from cedar
unraveling quietly from the red thread
that holds it together, I cannot mend.
The light and dark entwined.

Still believing
that to cradle a thing in one's own hands
calls it into being.

Delight and Mercy

"Those who seek outside themselves dream. Those who look inward awaken." —Carl Jung

In the dream I'm dancing with my mother.
Dancing close but clumsily.
I can't recall the weight of her arms on me
or her scent,
only her slippered feet
cemented to mine.
Pushing me earthward.

I don't remember my mother ever dancing.
It would take a robber in the house
or a saint
to get her to move with abandon.

I do remember her anger. Large as flame.
Engulfing the house. Emasculating my father.

Junior prom.
I'm slow dancing with a boy.
The Rolling Stones, too loud, on the radio.
I know all the words to the song, "Angie."
I know the nape of his neck.
The force of my arms around his thick waist.
The discomfort of his jeans rubbing against my smooth shaven legs.
His cheek soft as mink.

At our wedding
my husband and I waltzed
underneath the apple trees in Corralitos.

Unpracticed—
an awkward dance—
we stumbled.
Someone cut in.

Now my daughter covers my mouth
each time I start to sing.

Slow dances with her father.
Pirouettes determinedly
as their bodies move in unison.

Eucalyptus captures wind's song,
buzzing of bees a mantra,
woodpeckers tapping a rhythm.

Just yesterday
a bird entered our porch,
the window ajar
like a mouth wide open.

A young scrub jay
usually noisy
now fallen silent
where panicked talons touched screen.

After several minutes of this two-step
my husband intervenes.
Takes up a broom,
pushes ticklish tip to bird
who refuses to exit or surrender.

But my husband persists.
Brushes the jay past potted plants.
And now the door's wide open—
Still the bird's transfixed.

I want this poem to end
with a blue jay in flight.
My own small voice
like a delicate sparrow
urging him Heavenward.

Getting it Right

Everyone is either dying or being born.
I don't know them.
Or maybe I do.

My mother used to say
"You girls will be the death of me."
But I think it was my father who really killed her,
with his looks and his cheating.

I don't know my place on the wheel.
Am I coming or going?
I sew this burden to my chest, a multifaceted tattoo.
It's the depths of mystery, this time.
I can't know.

I envy the girls who have fathers, now aged, but smiling.
Heroic characters who once taught them how to drive.
Still debonair. White hair.
Bent slightly toward demise.
But my father was sad. Too sad to try.

His alcohol like a poison in my veins.
Like bitter medicine
I take in small doses to remember.

The way I would have looked at you.
Not for long, but shyly.
After you expired, ghost,
waxen figure, pale and bloated.

What I would say to you father, I've never settled.
Our relationship, a silence filling the universe
in the hollowed out spaces in my bones
where you aren't living.

What we could not say in this life,
can we speak it in the next?

The space between, father
is where I wanted to say.
How glorious it would be
to rest in the sun
or sit back in the shade
of a giant oak
whose hundred years test eternity
with the sap of consciousness
neither clouded nor old
not giving or taking
just solid and true.

I want to go back to knowing.
To slip beside him in the coffin, gently.
Whispers in the quiet church,
falling like leaves in autumn.

S.O.S.

Long after love left
my parents stayed together.
Breaking the rule that there was to be no fighting at dinner,
overturning plates, smashing tumblers.
Causing a peculiar kind of indigestion
that never left me or my sisters.

Battles as lengthy as days.
Weary childhood days I consider now,
reaching back in time to mend them.

Afterward, my father like a stone.
Grave as the delirious winter night.
Only the sound of percussive rain tapping on steamy windows.
When Moon lay low in the sky
and worried a message to me.

Then I wed words at the age of ten.
Releasing the sorrow that had sheltered me.
The way spring finally arrives whole.
Magnolia blossoms burst suddenly—utterly themselves.

Now I see my mother,
slender in her lace slip
before the gas stove
in the hollow yellow light of the kitchen
wooden spoon in her hand
stirring the pot slowly.
Tapping out an S.O.S.

Earth, My Witness

"I know the earth and I am sad." —Pablo Neruda

Once my father said
Earth loved me more than God.
He said there was nowhere to hide on Earth.
Planted corn and tomatoes in fresh ploughed Jersey fields.

Then I watched him talk to Earth
with his two large hands and the rest of his body.
Until she softened.
Until she sang and dreamed.

Once I walked the shores of Point Sur,
crying out to the spirit of Earth
and all those who had forsaken me:
my mother, father, teachers, friends and lovers.

Wind took my words,
let them go.
Earth, my witness.

I know the Earth.
Moist fertile fields like crying.
Backbone of trees; poplar, oak, and redwood.
Snowfall that covers everything, like sorrow.

The evening's mind huge.
The cry and paw of darkness
that dwells within me.

The sadness of Earth, my grief.
The brokenness of ordinary things,
clocks and glasses and strollers.

Strange habits of men:
Neglect, disdain and punishment.
Angry wars,

drones and bullets and pesticides.
Spinning cars and freeways.
Minefields, battlefields, barbed wire.
Explosions.

When I despaired, Earth held me.

And the loneliness of Earth
even among all the celestial bodies.
Mischievous moon hiding for days.
The sun too quick to flare in anger.
Errant meteors that stun the surface.

And the ocean, a quarrelsome lover.
Chastising Earth.
Bickering with her,
wearing her down.
Or rising up in frothy rage
to meet her unexpectedly.

Changing its mind over and over.
Calling out to Earth again and again.

After She Died

"The morning breeze has secrets to tell you. Don't go back to sleep" —Rumi

After my mother-in-law was dead for awhile
the house came back to life slowly.
The stunned silence receded
like hush and wrench of wave.

Dutiful daughters long at her bedside,
in-laws in the next room,
the many obedient sons.
Everyone moved around a little, breathed.

After she had been dead for more than a few hours
I wondered when my sister-in-laws would return.
But they vigiled over the body ceaselessly.

Drifting with her perhaps a little through the stratosphere.
Out to the edge of the galaxy;
Explorers of the darkness, with her now.

I was not a stranger to grief.
Some days it covered me like armor
no knife could pierce.
Other days it left me,
barely breathing.

"When I was a young girl, all I wanted was a pony,"
she had said
the last time we spoke.
Then she shot off without warning, at breakneck speed.

After the second day I began to wonder.
The Jewish wife, her youngest son's,
confessed it was creepy,
the body in the next room, mostly ignored now.

Occasionally I tiptoed in.
But I didn't find anything
I was looking for.

No luminescent angels playing gentle harp strings.
No brilliant white light.
Not even simple levitation.

Just a frail woman, ninety-four.
Eyes closed
in reverie.

I wanted to lie down with her.
Whisper something clever in her ear
or funny.
But I didn't.

On the third day someone called the funeral parlor;
her body destined for flames.
Someone else made dinner.

I scraped skin from potatoes.
Awkwardly washed vegetables.
Chopped onions.

Then her oldest daughter
lifted her from the bed.
Scrubbed her body raw and clean.

Outside the clematis clung to the vine;
Traveling skyward.

No one expected a miracle.
The way the women found the tomb of Jesus
empty on the third day.

No one expected she would return.
Yet everyone waited.

Metamorphosis

for L. W.

How long has she lay there dying
while the bleak world suffers not?
Low tide's sudden treasure—I gather shells while crying.

Last time I saw her—trying.
Was this really her lot?
To lay there long and dying.

All her children vying
to be the first, the last, to speak, to touch, to love—my stomach in a knot.
The seashells, plunder in my pocket lying

that this inevitable end is easy—after all it's time she's buying.
Only sleeps in morphine dreams gavottes.
How long she lays there dying!

When my time comes I want it quick, instead of brain cells drying
all systems shot
like broken seashells now I'm mining.

In birth and death the angels smiling
while she lies in silence on her cot.
How long has she lay there dying?
A cache of shells I bring her, spirit flying.

Resurrection

The coyotes cried all night long.
Or perhaps it was laughter,
sharp as sticks piercing the face of the moon.

My daughter sleeps soundly beside me
I can feel her dreams,
her blood churning through young veins.
Not stirring for coyote or anything else moving
in the forest.

The laughter of the coyotes
—I'm sure it's laughter now—
drifts in and out of my dreams.
I'm certain I'm sleeping now.
And then again I could be awakening.

The next morning our daughter spots the horse
solidly lying down in the meadow.
I am certain he is dead.
This explains coyote's laughter.

Next time I look out
the farmer has arrived with a wool blanket.
It's blue and white, large enough
to cover the animal's entire body.

I'm still certain it's dead though.
As I am certain I'm dead at age eight
when I fight sleep each night
for as long as I can.

I'm certain I am dead
when my father quietly moves the covers off the bed,
drifts in beside me,
smelling of tobacco, musk and tar
and whiskey, like fields of grain.

I'm certain I am dead
when he places his hands on my body.
Up and down the length of it
I shiver—like last breath.

Still I strain to hear his heartbeat,
his chest so close to mine.

This morning of the horse,
I pretend it's just another ordinary day.
I scramble eggs for my daughter in the cast iron pan.
Make strong bitter coffee.

I refuse to look out the window again.
Such a large animal.
How will they bury it?

It's my daughter who cries
"It's moving."
And I think she's dreaming.

But we both look toward the window
where we see—plain as day—
the horse standing tall and upright in the muddy field.
Its black medallion of a body glistening.

BECOMING

First Day of Summer

Eight years old and she has never seen the ocean.
Her family drives two hours from the city
in the shiny black Buick to reach the shore.

When they arrive
all but stuck to their seats
her father peels her off.

Makes her slip on flip flops,
bare feet not allowed.
He hates the sand.

She wants to be held by him,
but he hugs the burdensome cooler
filled with potato chips and beer.

She can see her mother's body but it is too far away to touch.
Can hear the seagulls' mocking call,
not sweet like the songbirds that eat from the feeder
back home.
She wishes she were there.

He takes her to water's edge.
Expects her to jump in like a slick fish.
She imagines viscous seaweed,
bad stew in her mouth and on her lips.

Would rather walk all the way home
on the hot asphalt concrete with sorry skin
than dive into this.

He insists that she swim.
Taunts her.
Easily pulls at her floral bottomed suit.

She hides behind her mother
who is there on the sand
but is not there.

Beads of sweat ring her face
and the back of her neck.
She prays for wind
to take her to another shore.

Communion

Already landed on the shore of desire
she must put on the white dress
freshly starched and hemmed
not straight but in a curve because her mother is a realtor
not a seamstress and her hands shake with excitement
for her youngest child
and from some small white pill to help her
unwind and a glass of white wine or some
combination—so what it is Sunday morning.

She has never been to a wedding
but today she is to be a bride.
In catechism the priest said she will marry Jesus;
that without any physical evidence
she must believe
that he loves her uniquely and completely.

She expects he will treat her kindly—
better than her father treats her mother.
She is ready to be a devoted wife—
as long as he does not shake
or beat her.

And in a wilder moment—when she allows
herself more hope even—
she wonders where they will go
on their honeymoon vacation.

She has studied that He is a fisherman
and thinks a cruise would be fine.
She likes the idea of eating fresh fish from the ocean.

Maybe she could be in a miracle and walk on water also.
Over the heads of her classmates she would float upwards,
buoyant like a runaway balloon.

The way she leaves her bed when her father
joins her at night
kicking back the cool sheets
awakening her sister
rearranging the animals with one fell swoop
a giant bird he descends.

While she pretends to ascend to the heavens
but only reaches as far as the bedroom ceiling—
hovering—a lost angel
where she watches his shenanigans
like television
but this is real
all quivering flesh and sex.

She wonders if Jesus will have three days worth of stubble
from not shaving after he has risen again.
And what it means to be dead,
the quiet of it like the darkness of sky at night
before the stars embrace light.
She wishes He will smell like pine forest
or cedar, her favorite tree.
Not the sweat of semen sticky on her lips
(God's secret) or the alcohol on her father's breath.

Maybe they can buy a house in the suburbs.
She knows Jesus is rich.
She has high hopes for her husband.
Even if she is only seven she can dream
she is at one with something.

Latchkey

We didn't know we were latchkey kids—
my sisters and I.
Stepping off the school bus at 3:45
walking past our neighbor's farm
with its dark bulls grazing.

The door unlocked
we'd strip off our plaid jumpers
and in our slips
and knee high socks
drink milk and eat graham crackers.

Four-thirty, we'd watch "Dark Shadows."
Never quite figuring how Barnabus Collins
could get out of being a vampire.

After the television trance
we'd be restless and cranky
waiting for our mother to come home.

Six o'clock we'd set the table:
Monday's meatloaf,
Tuesday's macaroni and cheese.

But we'd never know
when dad would get home
or if he'd been drinking.

Then we were hushed into silence,
living with our own private ghosts.
The groundskeeper who hanged himself in our barn.

The way our dad handled us.
The way he touched me and my sisters.
His little wives he fucked.

According to our mother
it was our religion that would save us.
The blessed cross.

The perfect moment at bedtime.
We'd kneel down, like good children, beseech God.
Say our prayers
pretend to believe.

Conflagration

On Saturday mornings my father burned our garbage
at the edge of our forty acre farm.
Down by the graveyard of old bottles
of Coca Cola and Mountain Dew.

I liked to watch him work.
The deliberate strike of the match,
and then the sharp flame leapt up.
Like our German shepherd nipping at the postman's heels.

I liked how the heat curled the labels inward
so that I could see the words *Millers, Budweiser* and *Chef-Boyardee* shrivel
finally.
The blaze turning crimson to indigo then yellow again
and the week's newspapers reduced to ash instantaneously.

My father seldom spoke, but for an occasional, "Stand back."
Dumbstruck, I listened, never asked a single question.
I understood this chore was solemn, unbearable.

Fighting back the wooded brush,
cutting a deep circle out of the earth
to keep us safe, contain the conflagration.

Sometimes the wind would kick up.
Then smoke would snarl acrid in our faces,
the smell like burning rubber.
Burnt remnants like whirling dervishes before us.

When it became too hot to stand it any longer
I'd back away, half watching, still curious.
My father, Prometheus, with a long handled shovel
sweaty and serious, staying with it, until the last spark diminished.

He'd be out there sometimes until mid-afternoon.
Long after I'd gone inside to my room.
This was slow business, his thirst for absolution,
his labor to make us clean and whole by Sunday morning.

Sunday's Money

Midway through the mass
my sister and I made a beeline
for the bathroom in the cold rectory
next to the stale kitchen.

Where volunteers make coffee for after
to go with sugary sweet donuts—heavenly
reward for suffering all the way through
the sermon and the transubstantiation.

In the stalls we *shush* each other and
Hurry, hurry, trying not to giggle.
Re-dressing as fast as possible, fishnet stockings bulging under
layers of clothing equal to nun's apparel
frigid Jersey winters.

We wait then in the aisle for the right moment
as the organ catches a low note—
its quarrel with joy—
And then return to the pews, awkward as any sinners.

Just in time,
our mother waiting, eyebrows raised, hands folded.
The collection basket—something shoddy and woven—
barreling our way.

As if on cue we toss in coins
to pay off sins from the week before with quarters and dimes
pilfered from our mother's purse
only that morning.

Or sometimes there's an envelope
filled with bills on special occasions,
Like Christmas or Easter or the Feast of St. Francis,
my sister named after him.

Then there are the votives
which cost a mere dollar.
Prayers said until the candle burns out.
Rubbed to the nub
the color of plum cherry.

Ash Wednesday

"All are from the dust, and to dust all return." —Ecclesiastes 3:20

We didn't know what it meant,
our foreheads anointed
for the second time in our short liturgical lives.
The first at Baptism with holy oil,
warm from the priest's sweating hands.

We were supposed to repent,
first day of Lent.
What had we done?
Spoken out of turn in class,
squabbled with a sibling.

But there were darker secrets
we couldn't even share in the confessional
involving not just our souls
but our precious flesh and bones.

I worried over mine
then deserted it
until many years later.

I cared more for the donkey of the story anyway—
a mule of stubborn peace.
The one Christ rode in on to Jerusalem
the day of the offerings of the palms.

These ashes made from palms
itchy and uncomfortable.
Marking us with sorrow and disappointment and sin
that hadn't even come yet.

In church I turned my neck
to see the processional
I would not be part of.

Self-conscious I would forget my turn,
drop the urn of magic ash,
tip the world
in someone else's favor.

September

Buster Brown Mary Janes, kneesocks and awkward
knit sweaters over dull brown jumpers
my mother handmade in duplicate.
My sister and I dressed like shy nuns.

My birthday fell
just before school began,
dread and anticipation in equal measure.

And Father Rodriguez, for eternity, looking to make a buck
to keep himself in shiny Mercedes
closed up his gambling operations in the rectory.

Clean now as my mother's kitchen—
mornings she baked muffins
to put into our lunchboxes:
"Felix the Cat" for me and "Dennis the Menace" for my older sister.

My father, always off to work early
to pick up other people's garbage.
As if we don't have enough of our own, my mother said.

Even at ten I wanted another life.
Wanted to follow the scarlet tanager south,
where the trees stayed plump and the temperature never plummeted.

I wearied of the eastern winter
even before it began.
Feeling the numb cold in my dumb bones.

I wanted to be more like my sister—
sour and confident.
Like someone I didn't know how to be.

Instead I was silent.
Surprised to be of this earth.
Like an animal caged for no good reason.

History of Undergarments

On wash day my mother always stripped down
to her underwear—Hanes—
not high cut or briefs or bikinis, just white cotton classic.

As a toddler I'd a fondness for Tinkerbell and Snoopy embroidered on the front
(size 4X).
And in kindergarten favored the ones with the days of the week embossed in
gold.
Or monogrammed with my initials, so I could wear them proudly, like a badge
or a testimonial.

In elementary school our names were monogrammed on all our clothing:
The brown sweaters and plaid skirts so we wouldn't mistake them
for another's in Physical Education.

Which is where I found out—in fifth grade—
that Minnette Grosso had already gotten a bra (furtive glances confirmed it)
while the rest of us were still in undershirts.
Still playing with Barbie Dolls and shunning boys completely.

When I got to middle school my mother warned me about sex—
Never take your panties off for anyone, she said.
But Susan Goldstein had given hers up already,

as the entire class witnessed on the steps of the American Museum of Natural
History.
A windy day in New York City,
a young brunette Marilyn Monroe in a floral print dress,

and her sex
blooming right there
on 79th Street and Central Park West.

Lipstick

A kiss of sweat,
a treat.
Halloween.
Desire.
Oval mouth shape frame,
hides pearly white smile.

Remembers
when the first tooth came and went.
Hugging the table
with a bite
and the jaw
and the anger
and sting,
like nettles in a field.

The trap of a mouth
ropes you in.
Steely, glittering, polished—
Gold, silver, enamel, porcelain—
a forest of jewels.
With lips as full as yours,
you should be wearing lipstick.

A Barbie mouth.
Pouting, polite,
parting to let him in
toward tongue's decay,
plaque on gums
despite the singing of floss.

Bacteria brewing
becoming a word.
The mouth washed with Ivory.
The bar wide and pungent.
Pure animate passionate hope
that what we say resonates.

Lip pressed to lip,
pressed to paper.
A row of colors—
each one more promising,
complementary.
Reds and oranges for olive complexions.
And fair ladies get pink's glossy light of morning.

Learning to Speak Poetry

I loved that Joey Fernandez put his tongue in my mouth
during seventh period when we were supposed to be
studying public speaking with Mr. McCarthy.

It didn't feel evil to skip another high school class.
Just a state of mind like *cool* or *in* or *happening*.

Like pulling out the chair
at the exact moment
David Rathbone went
to sit down on it.

His baby face slightly reddening
thick glasses partially askew
when he picked himself up
from the dusty floor

where Julie and her sister Nina
had planted chewing gum
the day before.

The janitor skipping our homeroom
—*animals live there*—
he was overheard saying.

Later that day Joey took me to his bedroom.
I stripped off my clothes
forgot my school girl manners.

Meekly protested.
After all, he was the one
who had carried my heavy bag

at the county fair
and spent all his hard-earned money
on cotton candy, the roller coaster and a stuffed zebra.

My girlfriends tried to talk me out of it.
He was *fast* they said.
A year older.
A Mexican.

But when we were alone in his shabby room—
bedcover ripped, furniture nicked—
his mother at work in the school cafeteria
his father off again, who knows where,

he recited poetry to me.
Verses whole from Neruda and Lorca.
Men I didn't care to know yet.
Men I would come to know better—exalt even.

Long after I had forgotten this boy who taught me to French kiss,
that year in high school when I became aware of my middle class life.
And first learned how lyrical the words, *I love you*, could be.

Rough Country

Sweet slick black haired Jimmy promising his sex,
my underwear wet at the thought of it.
"Watch it or you'll wind up pregnant," my mother said.

In sixth grade Father Thomas
diagrammed the act of penetration
and spat into the trash at each pause in his lecture,

the scent from the incense rising
from the rectory.

This was rough country,
above the timberline
where no trees grew.

But Jim's eyes were obsidian.
His salty skin the ocean.
When I went down on him
his scrotum like cotton candy in my hand.

Too shy to speak of it
we traveled in silence to this sacristy,
solemn initiates bearing neither grace nor ease,

following our instincts
the way pollen falls in summer
or mushroom spores,
rise up.

Chasing the Ghost of Yeats

Leaving my literary studies at the university grounds
I rode the bus downtown
on Friday nights
to the *Poet and Patriot Irish Pub*
a rock and roll bar
corner of Cedar and Maple.

Love's pearl
hidden under my polka dotted dress.
Spoon filled with desire
crisp bill rolled
up
waiting for the buzz
that informed the evening
inhabited my body.
Like the water we are made of
ocean of hoodwinked and silent stars
above.

Night dragged
on.
Paper thin stories,
Poker,
packs of Pall Malls.
Talk tangled like a vine.
I drank cheap wine
after the shots
to tamp down
the thump of my heart.
Sweet innocent organ.

I waited for the customers to thin out.
Waited to see who would be left behind
to travel on the tide with me
into Saturday morning.

Persimmons

Curse the passion that bears fruit
tender as pulp, limpid, divine.
More ornate than ordinary apples
when I was a child.
Trees of dizzying breadth and height
with one spontaneous gesture
could be fallen on the forest floor.

If men were like persimmons
you could eat their flesh raw.
But for tough skins
outer layer of machismo
this would be true.

Of all that matters
fruits' first flowers
perfumed sweet
then sickly to be spoiled
in an instant's deliberation
hesitation.

Persimmons so different—
knowing not the humility of carrots and sweet potatoes
languish unknowingly
become more feminine then
soft and malleable
ready for transmutation
in our two hands.

Fruits of our labor,
the gathering and the chopping
that no one should hunger
where it is safe to conjecture
over outcomes less subtle
than bread and muffins
and sometimes pudding
thick and wavering

and syrupy like affectation
or sometimes fallen flat in the pan.

If love were like persimmons
uncoerced fruit
would fall more frivolous
than apples in orchards
which are in need of netting
weighty with solemnity
uncreate.

A sticky sweetness to savor, persimmons.
Kiwis' alter ego.

Calamari Season

They wink at her
and across the water she sees open mouths
all toothy flesh to catch.

Sees cement battleships.
Hears coast guard
warnings.

Tonight eager fisherman cluster to make their squid kill
clever to mask smell of fish dread
with excitement and expectancy.

Yet having only two legs
she can't relate
to this world of eerie incandescence.
Nights all blue and electric.
No stars where they should assemble.

It traps her.
This harsh light falling
in squares along her bed.

She tries to recall now the
softness of afternoon colors
spawned from the same dome of sky.

Swoons for the sweetness of
summer's fluidity
not the hot glare.

Rush of autumn soon to follow
through an open window
and down her naked body.

Each ripple a sensation
wave of hand and sea
like tentacles exploring inkily.

With deepest ocean secrets open
she dreams a lover
fallen like Perseid meteors from the sky.

The offerings he makes, temporary, unspoken.
And in the morning the fishing boats are gone.

Invasion of the Sea Lions

They waited for night to fall.
Swam in while tourists were soundly sleeping.
Couldn't get into cafes or theaters fast enough.
Settled into restaurants,
They had no reservations.

Greedily they came
Flesh on flesh
Clumsy on beaches
Like new lovers.

Inside
Feel the pull of tides
Black as jet black night
Blackened, beckoned.

A dance, a ritual
This mating
Cleaving
Universal swing
Part violence
No romance
In and out like tides
Awkward
Pressed between flesh.

Come up for air
Find me
Your heart clamors
Survives
Through fog and mist and dreams
Like a sailor who knows how to chart stormy seas.

Mornings
I run from you
Try to blend in
But slippery with sweat

And glistening with sand
I can't escape,

Your heart beats
A drum
It anchors me
Unearthing
Up through tides
Swells
Larger and larger.

I can hear the sound all through the city
The yelping of small pups
The birth cries.

Remembering the Affair Years Later

In thin mountain air of August we scouted Shasta roadsides
the unadulterated joy of finding blackberries—an obsession.

Your sister had asked for some; given us pails to fill now
to be traded in tender for marmalade and jam later.

So we obliged her desire,
a unified force following bees
into brambled dense thickets.

You on your knees to the hunt
my arms and legs bared to thorns
relentless heat and bristling remorse.

Taps played as berries startled into buckets
ripe fruit, so tart and dark.

Our hands and mouths stained
with what we'd eaten.

INTO

Love Poem to the Universe

Did he really come from the other side?
And what did it mean
that God so loved the world
that He sent his only son?
If he loved the world so
why didn't He make the journey Himself?

The sun is a golden orb in my throat.
One way in—
Heaven or Earth.
When are we not happy to sit in a garden?
Eden, Gethsemani, Central Park.

Same thread of lightning
same star
binds us through the heart
to the Earth's slow comfort.
I can almost touch it now—
your hair, your breath, your visions
not unlike those of angels.

Once covered with momentary fires
the hills smolder
like the inside of the sun
cast out
long after we are gone,
having known both pleasure and pain.

Dawn's Early Light

You grope along the edges of night
waiting for day to rise up
as if challenging you to something.

You try to bridge the gap
between sleep and wakefulness.
Wait for your husband to stir
or songbird's first tentative, lonely note.

A rock in your throat
the same way you left it.
The muscles and bones of a body
you're still getting to know,
wild wisp of desire, unreachable.

You want to shout hello
but you don't know what you're after.
The sheer delight of air, echo of light.
You've got to get up sooner or later.

On the border of your consciousness
there's a song playing
traversing the familiar rundown
interior of your gray brain.

This is California so there's no more west to go.

Sometimes you can't believe it still matters:
Get up, put on your clothes…
What you eat for breakfast: a glass of orange juice, Cheerios.

Your daughter's lost another tooth;
she's waiting for the money under her pillow.
A wedding band on your finger
constant change and expectation.

Outside, dawn beckons impulsive
if you just follow her each minute.
Her lipstick red, her smile wide.

You remember the hawk you saw yesterday
who dove into the blackberry bushes—
hunting rabbits or moles. Emerging defeated.
Shrieking high-pitched anger, stopping to look at you.

Now you hear the hungry ghosts clamoring at your door.

Fear of Mountains

for Sharon

In this watchful valley I am not lonely.
In the shadow of the mountain
joined by a peacock's gaze
plumed feathers expanded to embrace
dance of delight on crusted snow with delicate feet
until a more showy flight sustained.

Truly this is not a dangerous place,
although the locals laugh
at the mention of an occasional ambling bear,
brown like the hills in summertime drought.
What would it mean to see one of those creatures
bounding through the meadow now?
Just another wild desire let loose upon this earth?

Whatever it is about mountains that frightens you
could be forgotten here.
Whether treacherous heights, God's grandeur, or our own diminution.
For the lake is quiet and tame
and more than once I could see the spirit of this place,
sunlight cradling her skirt of pine
as delicate as first Christmas.
Imagine a whimsical wind to lift like Canada geese
hopeful in journey.

Last night I dreamt of first crocus breaking through snow.
We each had our own garden and I could see your girlish face
expectant, wanting more than nature could give you.
Tell me, have I betrayed my home already
by loving this place with love's ardor
for what is new and still and kind?

Making Love to Oak

She stands outside the bedroom window
faithful as the rising sun to greet me
sometimes wanting
to come
to me
still mostly content in her quiet way
to watch me
and the hummingbirds' whir
traveling deep
to gather nectar
sucked up
from secret folds of summer orange flowers whorled.
She is a solace for nesting birds before they take wing.

I want to lie down in her deep gray folds of bark
wrinkled with age
curved like a racetrack for thoroughbreds
with lilt of breaking waves
she beckons.
And I want to lie down inside her
place my crotch on her crotch
swing and gyrate with the velocity of wind's abandon
mingle my sweet liquid sex stirred up with her seeping sap
peel the layers, strip her bare
flesh on flesh, skin on skin
until I penetrate to the very root
the heart of the thing.
The mystery where she is.

In summer she offers the green buds lasciviously
with outstretched limbs
all angles
buds round and hard
like nipples erect
small cones of sex
leaves lovingly waxed

with her own volatile oils
sweating in the afternoon heat.
Spilling over with secrets meant only for me.

A Love Poem

for Steve

I've never written a love poem before
but summer plays her girlish tricks
heats the blood in my veins so that it runs
like sap from your Vermont maples
sugar sweet and almost to boiling.

This warmth reminds me of Mexico.
The steady sultry pressure of promise,
hotel rooms with no Bibles.
Sex in the air there, heavy but no shame.

I miss you. This is the story trying to get out.
Making its way to find you.
Because the rhododendrons need watering
and I need inspiration.

Remembering all these years I dreamed you
and out of silence—great icy pool—you came
as if from another star and I from a distant planet
and my heart leapt up to greet your heart.
Every time I see you now the same.

Some birds mate for life but we could easily part ways.
Like water recedes for larger tides coming.
But this isn't my worse dismay.
Rather that we might not recognize the other.
Imposter selves rising up out of the shadows.

Oh, this is too close.
God knowledge.
The gestures you create.
Shape of your face.
Small sounds in sleep.
I don't think we are made for this on earth.

Before Work

I should have gone into the next room
and kissed my husband good-bye.
But anger is large in front of me
a wild animal I can't contain.

Our cat doesn't know.
He rubs his body across the thick midsection of my spouse,
the way I used to seek his bulk, back when we were courting.
The cat loves him innocently.
The way I once did.

Today it's the small things:
the way his toothbrush does not stand erect
in the holder in the bathroom.
Crumbs on the clean kitchen counter.
Just a smidgeon left in the bottle of jam in the back of the refrigerator.

It's still there, love, buried deep in the dark forest, along with desire—
Misplaced, the way you can't find your car keys or your winter hat.

It's always like that.
You pour yourself a cup of water—
drink a little, think you've had enough.
Later you return, insatiable.

It's the big things:
The way all my shortcomings are reflected back at me
from that figure in the bed, a reclining Adonis.
Eternity a chain that seems to wind around us endlessly, roping us in.

Fuck Jung and an army of psychologists!

For I am a stubborn mule.
Returning to the same pasture
again and again.
Even though the grasses are brown and dry
and there is nothing left to chew on
until the rains come once more.

In Lavender Fields

To cup my hands gently and full with you
I turned to earth—where else but home?
To lavender fields—the aroma a song,
Bees at the flowers our aggravated hunger.

I turned to earth and turned again.
The deep rich clay loam of it—your world.
Hungry for love's flowering I turned to look
Saw time, the tyrant, our own.

From clay loam I gathered shards.
The broken cup in my small hands.
Once filled so sweetly with you
Now godforsaken lavender fields.

Eve Reconsiders

When she stole the apple
she didn't know what she was getting into.
How rotten an eviction from Paradise
without any notice.

Sure Adam had his faults:
His blind obedience.
Constant dreamy smile.

Good looks aren't everything
she remembered someone
somewhere
once told her.

But God hadn't been such a bad landlord after all.
No brass knuckles to keep his children reined in,
just laughter that opened
into deep lakes and placid mountains.

Roses without thorns
Remorseless scent of perfume
Quick painless sunsets.

Now the ravenous mouths
and rheumy eyes of the babies.
Their wailing like sirens, ragged clothing to mend.
Moving endlessly through time.

Quarrel with Love

It's just an ordinary evening sky.
stars by the handful, cold coming on.

The Tudor brown house darkening,
Summer turning on her heels, readying to go.

I can't sleep.
Garland of dreams eludes me.

Remembering the emptiness of that other house
my father left when I was thirteen.

I was on the brink of becoming a woman,
loneliness already my story.

Remembering how he never said he loved me,
just that he was going—Keep your distance.

Then how could I expect to love,
ever really love, another man again?

"Roaming hands and eyes," my mother said of him.
Who needs this love anyway?

I do.
Two words crept out of my mouth,

shy song birds
on my wedding day.

Trying it out. Just to see how it feels:
to give oneself completely to another.

Still not knowing what it means.
Love like a knot, in my hair, in my throat.
A tangled passageway of intentions I've followed.

Midnight. Silence caresses the stars.
I watch and anticipate first signs of amber light.
Wonder if anyone in the world waits with me.

And I hear the sound of the universe
that startles even itself—
The moan and hum of aum.

And when I return to the warm room
I see my daughter,
curled like a perfect ball of silk in her bed.

Her thin slice of breath, I can hear,
almost see, a shock of light.
Closed lashes flittering like hummingbirds.

Thinking of Saint Francis

They say he spoke with animals.
They say he touched the birds.
That birds came to him and sat in his hand.
For myself, I've always wanted that.
Belief.

Outside our house a blue jay makes her nest.
Three or four baby birds,
all squawks and beaks.
I can't see them yet.
So like a prayer
I imagine them in their fullness later.

In the morning the mother bird brings a green berry for them to share.
Suddenly she looks so small against the rest of nature.
But she is quite fierce really.
Protecting them.
Using her voice,
even against the orange cat.

It's all we've got.
Our voice.
Words like home and here and peace.
This moment.
Love and loyalty.
Belief.

Forgiveness

My mother's faith follows me.
Helps me to reach Heavenward, when I am worried.
Pushes me to say prayers on first awakening.

But hers was a dark God of justice and hate.
The way my father was a somber judge
when my sisters and I had mis-stepped, time and time again.
His hand ready to mete out punishment.
My mother's words sharper though than the sting of his belt.

Loose. Loose. Let loose those bonds of accidental love.
For I love them still with a child's need and lack of logic.

Love like a miracle, a curse, a frozen tundra.
And backwards in time I would travel to love them some more.
To rub my mother's calloused feet with tenderness.
To hold my father's brutal left hand, without flinching.

To say, *I give you this now*, with arms extended.
Like a child's gift: *I give you everything.*

Daughter of My Heart

An old Chinese story describes how lovers are predestined to meet: An invisible red thread leads from one person to another, no matter how far apart the two may be, and although it may bend and tangle it will never break. Parents waiting to adopt from this part of the world have embraced this idea, similar to the Western notion of destiny.

"Which way's China?" I ask my husband.
I'm standing on the balcony of our seaside apartment
the mighty Pacific before us
calm now, sometimes howling.

Connected by an invisible red thread
that surely exists, like God and stars, the moon and summers,
tied to a slim ankle or a dainty wrist
making its mark, indelible.

Everywhere I go there are daughters like you.
So close they could be your sisters
or some distant relative you remember
deep inside you.

In my dreams I am swimming,
buoyant with my desire to get to you,
fear having left me,
hope holding me above water.

Daughter, born of wisdom, not passion
of the heart, not the womb.
Found forsaken
under a bridge
beside a freeway
in a market.

Crying among the turnips and peppers.
Still heady with the scent of that other world,
extraterrestrial.

Night after night
I invoke you to come.
But still you are a silent fish
swimming in the ocean
and I don't yet recognize you.

Chosen

When they handed me a baby—our daughter
in the lobby of a four star hotel
in Nancheng China
I felt I had
crossed over
a threshold.

Like in the old movies
the cinematic love stories
when the husband carries the wife
through the doorway
of their newly purchased
suburban home.

And I had crossed into something now.
Like Christ carried a cross
up the mountain
to the place
He was crucified.

The crowd jeering along the way.
(Death making ready for resurrection.)
No one, save for Veronica,
offering him her veil
to wipe the sweat and blood away.

It was the dawn, the beginning of something:
wet diapers, days at home,
a toddler's pebbled language,
a new tongue.

The ring around the tub growing mossier,
basket of buttons on the table,
burnt beans on the stove,
lingerie buried in my dresser.

But the beauty is
I did not suffer
for this love
as she clung to me
like no other.
I was chosen.

A shared memory of loss between us
The taste of pomegranate on our tongues.
Gypsy soup,
the saltiness of oceans.
The sound of mermaids and beluga whales
in our ears.

Light pouring in now,
my heart enflamed and raw—
Blake's vision of angels.
I could not stop
once this thing had been set in motion.

Did not stop
the descent
into becoming
something
other than
my small
ordinary
self.

Hope

Just try and give up hope.
Words caught in the throat.
Startled sparrow's hesitation before flight.

Leave joy behind, compassion on the periphery.
With hope a cloak no longer,
despair one shortened breath away.

Just how will you stop the young boy in the field
each ripe summer day
so eager to pick blackberries at the edge?

And what will you say to moon
when she asks you to love
(recklessly) again?

Plums in June

There's no such thing as a free lunch.
Unless you are a raven or a crow,
choice morsels roadside to choose.

Everywhere plums in June dispel truth of lack or poverty.
My eight-year-old knows the ripest by color, picks low hanging fruit.
Cautions me to wait for the others—
difficult this patience for things.

In our yard jays squabble over the fallen ones, leftovers.
Treasuring plump orbs.
Our cars and the sidewalks,
smeared with bloody juice.

Something about this color—mauve her favorite—
she paints unselfconsciously.
Dips her brush into it again and again,
as she conjures sunsets and rainbows.

Still I can't erase the picture of the homeless
men on downtown streets who look ready to snap
like the limbs of dead trees in dry summer.

Others marooned on their own separate island
retreat to the understory of the jacaranda
where the blossom's purple hues all but devour them.

At noon the hot dog vendor
(corner of River and Front)
makes me an offer:
Buy three, and the fourth one's free.

Poem Is Banquet, Poem Is Feast

My students want to know:
What makes good poetry?
I think, bread and potatoes, plenty of food in the cupboard.
A full stomach. Then vivid dreams. Attention.

Beginner's mind, I say.
Don't cross out. Take risks. Ask questions.
"How can one day be so many things?" one young mother wrote.
A Zen koan I'm beginning to unravel.

Make desire statements.
This is the place I stop
to censure the thought (I'm losing my Buddha mind).
No ideas but in things.

The thing is that truth set down on the page looks nothing
like the mind of illusion.
The magician's trick. Sleight of the hand.
Not knowing.

But I want them to know, fully.
The way sky shines
luminous
after July rain.

I want them to know.
Each word a jumping off place
to ecstasy or sorrow.
Nothing in between.

A poem is a morsel to feed the hungry.
A grain of kindness.
Water that permeates
unmovable stone.

Soul's Anthem

Alone I watched a host of swallows form a graceful line.
The meticulous timing of streamlined wings sharpening the shape of it.
Plucking insects from the sky I could not see
the way other birds might pick them
from dewy morning grasses.

Purple martins at sunset show off swan dives before retiring.
The way British sailors proudly displayed
their swallow tattoos.
The birds at the ready to aloft their souls
to the next world if need be.

Now in bed with you—pomegranate sheets against your fair skin—
my mind keeps returning
to the agile antics of birds.
And I dream we've descended to a more youthful time.
My love for you broadening the scope of flight.

The years echoing the song of swallows:
Liquid, warble, twitter, hum.

Summer Solstice

My love, can you see through
to the realm of light?

Past even the point of longing and desire?
Where nothing is evil or vacuous or unknowing.

The wilderness inside my heart opens here—
where first birds spool songs from air

and sunflowers shake their thick lustrous heads
unburdening sleep and uncertainty with bright vision.

Our garden's yet a promise this year—
tendrils of sweet peas, patchwork pieces from last season,

a volunteer tomato here, a teetering stalk of chard.
But the flowers hold on greedily, alstroemeria, statice and yarrow,

as if in a daydream of chance and astonishment,
in love with you too.

Just Enough

Growing up we had no neighbors
only a thicket of pine forest
surrounding our house on all sides.

My grandmother up the dirt road didn't count—
except for Saturday night sleepovers
with my cousins Patsy Jo and Toni Ann.

Three ten-year-old girls swimming in her antique mahogany bed.
The sour face of the Christ looking down on us
as we watched a Disney movie, snacked on potato chips and anisette
cookies.

These days I can hardly watch T.V., with its astonishing news.
Floating cities—not romantic like Venice, Italy—
but Houston and Beaumont, Texas, submerged

everything we know
drifting.

And on our coast tenacious fires emblazon sky haze;
the sun, a brilliant ruby, far off.

In the still heat of this Indian summer night:
crickets camaraderie a choir, dancing dark bats, crystalline stars,

I hear my neighbors talking on their deck
their small pools of laughter, just enough.

Acknowledgements

It is with much love and deep gratitude that I wish to thank those who have helped me along the journey that became this book.

Gail Black, for listening.

William Everson, for "Birth of a Poet."

David Swanger, Tilly Shaw and Robert Sward, esteemed professors at the University of California, Santa Cruz.

Patrice Vecchione, for showing me how it's done.

My biological sisters: Patricia and Cheryl. And my mother and father.

My heart sisters: Suzanne Jones, Violet deLuna, Georgine Balassone, Tara Lumb, and Kristina Parkinson.

The Montagnes! Margie, Julie, Marc, and Dave, for family; and the late Marjorie Montagne.

Michael Pogrowski, Lynn Rebbeck and their extended family, for providing me with home.

My neighbors and friends, Beth Tarcher and Richard Hoover, for being there.

The Warren family, especially Lorraine and Rodney, for writing with me and caring.

The Bay Tree Bookstore family, for letting me grow up with you in the redwoods—especially Pamela Ackerman, Mary Raffanti, Rick Rudman, and Brian O.

ETR folks—eight years without windows! Cori Kocher, Laura Norvig, Mary Hegeler; and Kay Clark for your unwavering encouragement.

JRB, for helping me understand, and for the mountain.
Joan Rose, for reminding me about the angels.

All my students at the Community Poetry Circles, both in Santa Cruz and in Campbell, for allowing me to hear your new-born poems; especially Cathy Brasher, Lee Berman, Emily Bording ,Thea Crossley, Meaghan Donovan, Dick Green, Kate Hitt, Joyce Keller, Mark Loring, Julie Maia, Pamela Papas, Sheila Siegel, Joan Rose Staffen, Carol Stoneburner, Laurel Maxwell, Rose Meyers, Ruth Mota, Bernice Rendrick, and Juanita Usher.

Cheryl Gettleman and Thomas Riordan for reading the manuscript and writing with me.

Lisa Simon, for Squaw Valley!

Suzanne Jones, Kim Nelson, Maggie Paul, Lisa Simon, and Carol Stoneburner for the writing group at Tree Frog Lane.

My workshop teachers: Ellen Bass, Robert Bly, Deborah Diggs, Robert Hass, Dorianne Laux, Joseph Millar, Sharon Olds, Deena Metzger, and Len Roberts, for teaching with love, wisdom, and encouragement.

Catherine Segurson for Catamaran and T. Mike Walker for the Santa Cruz Art League.

All the folks at the assisted living facilities who lovingly help me create during the WisdomVerse[SM] workshops; and John Fox and the Institute for Poetic Medicine for believing in and supporting the work.

Snowshoe, my cat, for love; and Dr. K. for taking care of him and finding poetry.

An east coast native, **MAGDALENA MONTAGNE** moved to California to attend the University of California at Santa Cruz and has lived on the west coast ever since. A poetry teacher and workshop facilitator for students of all ages, Magdalena brings Community Poetry Circles to libraries in Santa Cruz County and her WisdomVerse^{SM} program to residents in assisted living facilities throughout the Monterey Bay area on California's central coast. Magdalena also works as an editor and book coach, and teaches ongoing, private poetry workshops at her home. She lives in the Santa Cruz mountains with her husband and daughter, and their cat, Snowshoe. Find out more at www.poetrycirclewithmagdalena.com.

www.ingramcontent.com/pod-product-compliance
Lightning Source LLC
Chambersburg PA
CBHW021152090426
42740CB00008B/1052